The Ballad of
Worple Road

"Where this idea came from, I don't know.
Why I started on it, I don't know. Had I
realised the tortures of word and line and fact
contortion that I would have to survive,
I doubt I would have started."

Max Robertson

The Ballad of
Worple Road

A Poetic History of the Early
Wimbledon Championships

Max Robertson

Foreword by
Sir Peter Ustinov

Illustrations by
Loon

Queen Anne Press

A Queen Anne Press book

Text © Max Robertson 1997
Illustrations © Alasdair Hilleary 1997

Max Robertson has asserted his moral right under
the Copyright, Designs and Patent Act, 1988
to be identified as the author of this work

First published in Great Britain in 1997 by
Queen Anne Press
a division of Lennard Associates Limited
Mackerye End, Harpenden
Hertfordshire AL5 5DR

A CIP catalogue record for this book
is available from the British Library

ISBN 1 85291 578 1

Cover designed by Design 2 Print
Reproduction by Leaside Graphics

Printed and bound in Great Britain by
Butler & Tanner, London and Frome

Contents

FOREWORD
BY
SIR PETER USTINOV

Max Robertson has long been a glittering star among sporting commentators, but life is as full of surprises as ever. Who could have guessed that behind the measured prose that tennis freaks like myself had come to relish, there lurked a poet? Not merely a poet, but an epic poet! Suddenly, the now international battlefield of tennis, with its huge rewards and wonderful uncertainties, has acquired an Iliad of its own, a poem stretching to a generous 1500 lines of carefully selected words, with as much rhythm as a baseline rally between champions. I must admit to my amazement at this achievement, since it only sings of Worple Road, the original venue of the Wimbledon Championships, by now as remote and legendary as the Trojan War. It stands to reason that, like Homer before him, Max is far too young to have known much of what he writes with such conviction, but their styles are often extremely similar. Who wrote,

Ye gods! Oh why, oh why did they conspire
To make the Champion victim of their ire
And bring about such monstrous verdict dire?

Obviously Homer, on the death of Hector. Wrong, Robertson, on the defeat of the reigning champion, Mrs Lambert Chambers, by Suzanne Lenglen in 1919, by a ball which hovered a long time on the net before deciding to fall on the wrong side, clearly the work of the gods.

Tennis is worthy of such celebration. From its courtly beginnings as a royal pastime there survive a few Real tennis courts, racquets of sorts, and the word 'service', the most venerable survivor among words in general use. It is astonishing to witness serves such as those of Sampras or Ivanisevic today, match-winning weapons, and then to reflect that it was beneath Henry VIII's dignity to merely set the ball in motion for a rally, so he called out a languorous but peremptory command, "Service!", and a domestic cautiously patted the ball to where His Majesty's opponent was sure to be able to reach it.

There are other historical precedents for the game which Major Clopton Wingfield so successfully transported into the open-air, and which the uncertainties of the weather have successfully reintroduced to covered courts. Apart from real-tennis, fives is another ancestor worthy of note, since the French Revolution was launched during a stormy meeting without a referee in the hall of the *Jeu de Paumes*, or 'Game with the Palms of the Hands' in Paris. Recently I was driven round Winnipeg by a charming young lady who was revealed to be the present World Champion of Racquets, a game which, in spite of its name, turned out to be played with the gloved hand, fives in fact.

Max, at the beginning of his Odyssey, hints broadly at the amatory implications of the invention of lawn tennis under the new but impermanent name given it by Major Wingfield. In yet another passage reminiscent of Homer, he writes:

> *'Sphairistike', the Greek for skilled ball-game;*
> *A game that seemed determined hence to prove*
> *Itself as ultimate arch-ploy of love.*

I can testify to the truth of this, having met my present wife on the tennis court. It was a game I would prefer to forget, because I was incapable of keeping my eye on the ball, but which turned out to be memorable all the same, because of her presence, for the time being on the other side of the net. In fact, despite my love of the game, I am not really the man to write such a foreword, since I abandoned poetry for prose when I was $13^1/_2$ years old. I recognise the moment so precisely because of a school report. "More was expected of his $13^1/_2$ years," it read, about a poem of mine entered into a competition. You will understand why I approach both Homer and Max Robertson with a certain trepidation and colossal admiration. The metric system is not one I was born with. This only affects my opinion, not my appreciation.

The ferocious and frenetic drawings by Loon are a great asset to the scintillating wit of the text, and the valediction to Dan Maskell is a moving genuflexion in the direction of a friend and colleague, the Nestor of this Epos. "Oh, I say" he used to exclaim; but when a player had just double-faulted when 0-30 in the final set, he invariably declared with the gravity of a High Court judge, "That could prove to be a very expensive mistake indeed".

The book ends with a stirring paean to Fred Perry, 1905-1995, well deserved, an indomitable figure in the history of the game, who, together with the unsung Bunny Austin, still alive at the time of writing, gave the Davis Cup to Britain for four shining years. But that is the stuff of future cantos from the hitherto secret pen of Max Robertson.

London
19th October 1996

AUTHOR'S PREFACE

My memories are many of Peter Ustinov in the varied guises of his genius, but my outstanding early one is of sitting beside him in the dressing-room of the RAC after a post-war game of squash. He was an unforgettable figure, profuse with sweat, anecdote and his own exceptional charm. I have always regarded him as the compleat all-rounder of intellect – brilliant writer, actor, mimic, raconteur, wit and above all human being. His addiction to lawn tennis is well known and the fount perhaps springs from his realisation that as a player he has his bounds, so loves to watch those whose skills, if woven into a single tapestry, might qualify for perfection.

Perhaps I am sentient to this definition, for I had much the same feeling when commentating on great players, always striving to picture their game accurately for the listener. That Sir Peter has now done me the honour of his foreword – and in such heart-bursting terms – is a gift I shall always treasure, if scarcely believe.

His tribute is weighty on the scale of gratitude but there are many others, to whom I owe the deepest thanks. There is no order of merit in unsolicited help and support, so my best course to steer seems to be the logical one.

Pat Savill, a talented artist, has shared so much of my recent life and so has suffered – not for the first time – a considerable load of the ballad's gestation. This, and the temperamental outbursts, she has borne stoically and she has always encouraged.

My son Martin inspired me in his own quiet way when, having been shown an early draft, he said, "Yes, that could be fine when you've had a chance to polish it". How right he was and how agonising that polishing has been, especially of the first 200 lines, written two years earlier in imperfect iambic structure. I hope he'll now feel the job is done, but I doubt it, for he has very high standards.

My daughter (and Elisabeth Beresford's) Kate has for years been a writer, disciplined to the urgent needs of an amazing cross-section of clients. She has been a marvellous staff of secretary, typist and critic under one brow, feeding my unreasonable and never-ending demands for "another - positively the last - small correction" in my miserable Virgo's ceaseless search for a perfection that too easily becomes corrosive. Marcus, Kate's brother, is owed much thanks for his forbearance of my out-of-court use of his firm's equipment – as are the various kind people on his staff who conveyed unceasing messages to Kate.

Once again Buzzer Hadingham, ex-chairman of the AELTC, who conjured an inspired verse 'The 100th Wimbledon' that we broadcast and I later used in the final edition (1987) of my history of the Championships, has been of enormous help. He was in considerable pain awaiting a hip operation but still gave the text a thorough examination, making some very useful suggestions, which I did my best to carry out.

Alan Little, the Museum's Librarian, has been a wonderful ally and point of reference: though busy with his own work, he was always willing to research some esoteric fact. He, too, has trawled through the manuscript for inaccuracy and fortunately netted but two very minor slips. I suspect his head must have dropped on his arms once or twice, for there was a vast shoal of facts to check.

Larry Hodgson, an ex-BBC colleague, who now annually runs Radio Wimbledon, which throughout the fortnight does a wonderful job in entertaining and informing the incoming and outgoing public, was kind enough last year to give me the freedom of the air for a daily recitation of one canto or another. Frew McMillan, superb two-fisted doubles player and commentary-box colleague, has prospected diligently on my behalf.

Lord Aberdare, President of the Tennis and Rackets Association, gave his blessing to its secretary, Brigadier Andrew Myrtle, circularising members with a publisher's leaflet, which drew surprising responses. The most interesting was from Colonel George Gibbs, who reminded me that once, in a trial squash rackets commentary on a match between him and a player known (not always affectionately) as 'Bummer' Scott, I had said, "Mahomet has gone to the Mountain". Despite not forgiving this, George has been untiring in drumming up support in the Winchester area. Another supporter is David Godfree, son of that great champion Kitty. He likes to get his oar into a cause, and he has – this time to effect.

Chris Gorringe, the Club's Chief Executive and Basil Hutchins, the Museum's chief, and their staffs have been, as usual, unobtrusively helpful, as have Sally Holdsworth of the ITF and the staff of the LTA under its Secretary, John James. Simon Elmes and Sir Roger Cary, both BBC, have been great allies. Peter Jackson, who on behalf of the Committee, has been in charge of the new No. 1 Court works, liaising with Mike Bridges, has done his utmost to find me backers.

John Parsons, the distinguished *Daily Telegraph* correspondent, has been most supportive. His predecessor, that great doyen of the Wimbledon press, Lance Tingay, who sadly died some years ago, and John Barrett, were a solid source of reference with their authoritative books. However, Alan Little and I take issue with Lance on one point. He says that Hadow, the unexpected Champion in 1878 when on leave from Ceylon, was a 'coffee' planter, whereas most opinions say 'tea'. In any event, once Loon's superb drawing of Hadow has been seen, he could not have been anything else but a 'tea' planter.

Which brings me full moon to 'Loon', Alasdair Hilleary. A passionate devotee of the great H.M. Bateman, Loon has his own most definite style and sense of fun. I am very lucky to have him on my side, introduced by old friends Roger and Christina Wellesley-Smith. Adrian Stephenson, my publisher, and I think we were unfeelingly fortunate when Loon snapped an Achilles tendon – ironically playing tennis – just as, we suspect, he was about to take evasive action on his beloved Scottish moors. This literally tied him to his easel at the *moment critique*, though with the handicap of not easily being able to reach it.

So to Adrian. What decided him to back such an obvious outsider? Verse, what could be worse; tennis, not a brilliant ride; an unsung 81 year-old poet – some jockey! He told me he liked the title. I hope he had better reason than that. His normal imperturbability is a great crutch. Mind you, his red hair is not entirely belied. I have given cause for its fire once or twice but hope I am now forgiven.

Now to the substance. The 'Ballad', in uneven verse, as I've said, was begun in early 1994. I did not get down to it again until well after moving to my seventh floor flat overlooking the Club in March 1995. Here, I have had the amazing experience of watching the new No. 1 Court character at an astonishing rate. Even more amazing was the clean-up, face-lifting operation that presented a wholly unruffled appearance for Wimbledon 1996.

Since then the work has gone on steadily and as I write the court (the grass was laid down last summer and will be vintage quality by the opening in 1997) seems complete, lacking but a few finishing touches here and there. Two other new courts have been born and work on the TV building is well advanced. It is clear that the whole site and area will serve the Championships magnificently, if less intimately and haphazardly than of old.

All this planning is due to the foresight and courage of the Championships Committee. The construction is under the aegis of the experienced TRY company, which has long carried out the Club's larger works. It built the old No. 1 Court, which opened in 1926, and which the company will demolish. This will allow the Centre Court to be properly completed with extra seats on its East side. In the new available space there will be a large Facility Building embracing the Members' and Competitors' Enclosures as well as special areas for the press, referees, umpires and other officials.

In charge of the TRY construction is Mike Bridges. How his mind is able to grasp and retain all the complexities of this huge operation I do not know. Mike always seems to have an answer to the myriad questions that a string of supplicants ask. It is delivered in the briefest possible terms. Time is too precious. Mike regains his 'main' at weekends, inevitably indulging his beloved sailing.

Seeing this growth, with daily reminders by huge cranes that seemed to be swinging into my windows, I was inescapably drawn to watch the mesmeric action, at times almost convulsive, when diggers ('grabs' as I call them) were performing in teams like terriers digging out an earth.

I was immediately reminded of a TV programme I had lately seen about the Great African Rift – hence the title of the first sonnet in the sequence that all this awareness inspired me to write, this sequence which is, in a sense, its own celebration of the great festivities that will be the centrepiece of the Opening Day of the 1997 Championships.

The Great Wimbledon Rift

Famed Wimbledon, the Koh-i-Noor of tennis,
The aspirant's dream diadem and sceptre,
Composes new illuminated chapter
In terms that seem to token dire menace…

The brazen vintage year of ninety-five
Sees Ra the searing sun-god flay the earth
To strip the flesh from soil and supine rock
With molten fire, in cataclysmic shock,
The waters of a giant stadium's birth,
Designed to clasp an emerald in its gyve…

This latest progeny a signal son,
Endowed with ev'ry part the gods could give
To serve its acolytes and so to live,
Henceforward to be known as Number One.

The Cranes

With supple majesty the titan cranes
Advance, retreat and pause in minuet;
Gyrate again, once more to skirmish; yet
Well fixed within their sky-high arcs and planes,

They never breach the tenets of their craft
But raise or lower loads with fluent ease,
Responding with precision to decrees
Of pilot hands, and effortlessly waft
Prodigious weights across the empty sky:
Thence, steered by signs from wheedling red-back ants
Each scrupulously drops its freight and plants
Another prop; then hies away once more to ply.

These courteous cranes do overlord the scene;
They swing to conquer, never to demean.

The Grabs

Below obsequious genuflecting grabs
Do grovel, scrape and, servile to their lords,
Play busybody parts with urgent greed.
Their jaws, like claws of elongated crabs,
Attack the soil within the shoring boards;
They scour and scoop, then spin to answer need
And fill a lorry-load or hole in ground:
They knead and smooth, solidifying space,
Manoeuvring with a sly sinuous squirm:
Their animated glee as if they clowned,
And playful gesture might e'en yet misplace
But 'tis the driver's will that doth affirm.

These digger denizens that roam The Rift
Incessantly ransack to shift and lift.

AUTHOR'S ACKNOWLEDGMENT

Many people have helped me. Some have shown such faith in the ballad that they have pre-subscribed the book (at healthy discounts I hasten to say). This is a precious balm to the anxieties of publishing and it has the added advantage of stimulating word of mouth echo.

I am so grateful to all of them, large or small. My gratitude is particularly felt to Peter Ferbrache, an old Guernsey friend.

In alphabetical order, those pre-subscribing to publication at the time of going to press are:

Canon UK
Coutts Group
Sir Roger Gibbs KBE
Guardian Direct
Legis Corporate Services
Lynn Collins Associates
Manchester Tennis and Racquet Club
Parmley Graham
Philips Electronics UK
Winchester Tennis and Squash Club

The Ballad of
Worple Road

Canto I   *Love All – The Seed is Sown*

Victorian days remarked the leisured classes
Engage pursuits, not followed by the masses –
Charades and billiards, fabricating rhymes
To playing croquet, or such garden pastimes –
All necessary 'form' for idle play
In gilded hours giving golden day.
Young gentlemen meandered round the lawns
Of country seats, oft dissipating dawns
In daring silver dalliance with young damsels
(Expert deceivers of their dragon mam'selles),
Conniving at clandestine assignations
So causing compromising situations.

And lo a saviour rode on to the field.
A yeomanry blithe major, Clopton Wingfield,
In winter of 1873
Produced a garden pastime. Thus did he
'Invent' lawn tennis giving it the name
'Sphairistike', the Greek for skilled ball-game;
A game that seemed determined hence to prove
Itself as ultimate arch-ploy of love.

No longer the decorous draw of croquet
With never slightest chance of hokey-pokey.

"CHARGE!"

"ANYONE FOR 'STICKY'!"

Oh yes, the lady could adeptly bend,
But glimpse of ankle that might well offend
Was not vouchsafed to ranging eye of flirt,
She having no real cause to raise her skirt.
But Sphairistike now – 'Sticky' for short –
Gave positive scope all around the court.
The chase of ball, the forays storming net
Provoked no hindrance and not even let

To titillating chance of sudden *crise*
Arising from "Yours – no mine!" – *Quelle surprise*!
A clash of rackets – then a well-bred scream…,
She stumbles, falling as in wishful dream…
His ready arm gives vigilant embrace
And suddenly they find they're face to face.
With kind opponents' quiz, no time to kiss,
But glances to each other promise bliss.

" YOURS …NO MINE ! "

Wingfield was swift applying for his patent,
Foreseeing quick commercial profit latent
In variform diverting garden games
Good families would play in their domains;
But all with racket and ball, soft or hard,
Derived of tennis true sung by the Bard.
Réal or royal for the cloistered game
As played by monks of French historic claim
(Its origins mislaid in myst'ries old),
A kingly gift of balls at 'Cloth Of Gold'.

Such previous pastimes of adroit invention
Are far too numerous in here to mention;
But one particular close antecedent
Lays claim to being somewhat better credent
As first performance of a garden game.
'Twas credited to Major Harry Gem,
Who with close colleague, a J. B. Perera,
Was founder of a novel sporting era.
They played a racket game on grassy lawn
In '72. Thus they saw the dawn
Of 'lawners' in their club at Leamington.

'Tennis' the word accepted now as one
With *"Tenez!"* Stand prepared, the game's begun.
For scoring, clock time seemed *à propos* choice
To chime off quarters as the umpire's voice.

At *forty* all just 'Deuce' announced score level
(Corrupt *à deux* – not plea to tennis devil).
And lastly 'love', so dear to pleasant play,
Corrupted, too, from *l'oeuf*, so purists say.
An egg deposited by hen or duck
Betokens nought – you're *roundly* out of luck.
Which is why when the swain pursues in chase
He's often forced retreat, egg about face.

"I THOUGHT OF IT FIRST ..."
"NO YOU DIDN'T ... I DID !"

The 'Sticky' game born in '73
Soon had *succès* quite *fou* for all to see.
'Twas called *lawn* tennis to discriminate
From ancient court game born of *real* estate.
Its acolytes true multiplied apace,
And soon found need for less restricted space.
T'was then a man of far prophetic foresight
Did seed the saga (soon to blossom bright).
Predestined man for fateful hour at hand,
Was on committee of a chosen band
Of croquet zealots who'd pursued their code
Since '70 within their Club's abode
At Wimbledon-Without, off Worple Road.

" HAVE YOU HEARD ABOUT THIS NEW
GAME 'LAWN' TENNIS OLD BOY ? "

" WOULD YOU LIKE A ROLL, MISS WALSH ? "

One int'resting small fresco in relief
Was gift by John Walsh, Editor-in-Chief
The Field, wherefrom the Croquet Club took fief,
Of pony-roller in '71,
Exchange for daughter joining in the fun –
By means of this first gratis membership,
The subject often of a weighty quip,

To be observed as still a figurehead
Of Centre Court when Worple Road was dead.

A timely innovator, Henry Jones,
A surgeon specialist with soothing tones,
Had thought for future growth so made no 'bones':
Aware a formidable foe's arrival,
He swiftly seized the pass-key to survival,
Proposing an enticing invitation
To join the two in close amalgamation,
So giving both a memorable hub -
'Th' All England Croquet And Lawn Tennis Club'.

Canto II   Volley, Lob and Service with a Smile

So fast did sporting lawners' int'rest grow,
That Jones and cronies made resolve to sow
A tourney's seed now recognised worldwide,
The Champion diadem of greatest pride.
This genesis of Wimbledon's pure heaven
Arose in year 1877.
They blazoned meeting for a contest true,
Accepting challenge from just twenty-two.

They drew up rules derived from royal tennis.
The height of net soon proved itself a menace:
Suspended from five feet to just three three
It stopped the baseliner from feeling free
To play frustrating passing shots – a flaw
Exploited cleverly by Spencer Gore,
Who served (roundarm the rule) with spin and slice,
Was up at net in less than just a trice
And then dispatched th'inevitable shot
By volleying from side to side the lot.
His ruthless tactic carried all the way
To final match postponed for cricket play –
The Eton versus Harrow game at Lord's,
Then signifying more in sporting records.
A colleague of seer Henry's, Cecil Marshall
Was proven foe for Gore to next assail.

Fair moniker for bull assaulting net,
As if intent on getting back a debt,
Gore swamped his advers'ry, who gained no more
Than seven games – a miserable score –
So hero Gore – 6/1, 6/2, 6/4.
T'was fitting Gore should be first Worple Champion
For *he* was born a son of Wimbledon.

'GORE BLIMEY!'

Next year Gore's play induced the full Committee
To lower net height merely inches three;
Still not enough to furnish stimulus
To passing shot, so leaving more or less
The same advantage to those angled volleys,
Which swiftly killed returns that seemed like dollies.
Subscribing royal rules, then Gore as Champion
Awaited challenge of the winner from
The fray of the All-Comers pre-event.
He proved to be a most surprising gent.
Tea-planting stalwart from fair isle, Ceylon,
Returned on leave, he soon had lit upon
This newly started sport, the garden rage,
So, quite by chance, transforming Hist'ry's page.
When introduced by old friend, Lestocq Erskine,
He liked the game and soon became so keen
He fast improved, then took up Erskine's 'dare'
And entered Wimbledon straight then and there.
There was no 'qualifying' horror then,
All avenues awide to gentlemen.
So gallant knight, young planter P.F. Hadow,
Unseated all contestants, th'only shadow
His conquest in the final of the same
Friend Erskine, who had first inspired his game;
His fourth round victim, Cantab A. T. Myers,
Not held as one of most distinguished fliers.
His claim to notice that he made a start
In newly legal over-arm serve art.

'ANYONE FOR TEA?'

The sage spectators of the Challenge Round
Had gleeful gathered, betting pound on pound.
The issue seemed assured for, come the crunch,
Could novice upstart now withstand the punch
Of those deft volleys? Would he, rather, crumble
Before their onslaught, hapless and so humble?
Gore charged to net as all had predicated,
But his opponent now initiated
His own device to deal with lethal volleys.
He lobbed returns and lengthened out the rallies,
So giving Gore a castigating chase
That had him scuttling back askew to base.
Score "7/5, 6/1, 9/7 – Hadow!"
Indeed, it was a triumph for the tyro –
The first to win without a loss of set,
A punter's long-odds dream to win such bet.

An asterisk to destiny's romance!
Young Hadow almost wrecked his Champion chance,
Inanely pierced by shaft of strong sun-arrow,
Supporting dear loved alma mater, Harrow,
In annual cricket match played versus Eton
At Lord's, so feeling sick and nearly beaten.
However, his robust Victorian schooling
Enabled him, despite this witless fooling,
To vanquish impotence and so fight through
Two finals, gaining thus his glorious due.

T'was true, from practice for the Challenge Round,
His rival, Holder Gore, was also found
Experiencing a minor handicap,
His wrist so strained it lacked its normal snap.
All this, of course, is purely by the way,
For as we know young Hadow had his day.

Forthwith, attaining thus his self-made wager,
He left the scene free for an older stager,
Reclaimed to planting tea in far Ceylon,
Not once again to be observed upon
The Centre Court until the Jubilee,
With Champions summoned by the Club's decree,
Receiving medals of commemoration,
Providing nucleus of celebration –
All taking place at Church Road, Wimbledon,
Then Worple Road the tennis 'Hambledon'.

Reverting to the '70s, year 9,
The entries doubled, as the tennis vine
Took firmer hold. A sporting young divine,
Most personable parson J.T. Hartley,
Deserted Yorkshire parish and then smartly
Was victor in four rounds of first week matches –
A fine performance, but for sure t'catch is –
An upright man with strong faith in the Lord,
John Hartley hastened forth and sprang aboard

The Northern Flier, which in that strict day
Was fast and never prone to drear delay.
He preached a sermon stimulant with verve,
The text propounded, *"They* who also serve".

" AMEN ! "

Refreshed by pulpit, back then fast to court,
And to All-Comers' fray without a thought:
But handicap, yes, of a ten-mile drive
In pony-cart to catch express, arrive
On time to play but famished, scarce alive.
He lost first set in semis to Cec Parr
And seemed to be a goner, fading star;
But Heaven intervened with timely rain
And Hartley, taking tea, regained his main,
Result 2/6 6/1 6/1 6/1.

The Powers guaranteeing right so done,
Had Hartley now in mind for final fun.
His foe was dark horse V. St. Leger Goold,
Whom, come this day, his spirit over-ruled.
'Twas well Goold's name was never then inscribed
Upon the Champion's roll. It was proscribed
For *he* committed murder foul in France
And scarce escaped the gallows' ghoulish dance –
Correctly, p'raps, the guillotine's sharp knife.
Instead was banished, serving out his life
Confined and stranded lone on Devil's Isle,
Perdition for an act grotesquely vile.

' THE GAME IS UP ! '

Canto III   The Pirate and the Smashing Renshaws

1880 begat the service let,
Attracted also strongest entry yet.
Full sixty aspirants arrived at net,
Reduced at posts to an exact four feet,
A change base addicts avidly did greet.
Herb Lawford, doughty ever-keen contender,
Subdued all comers but then gave surrender
To Champion Hartley in the Challenge Round,
Yet doggedly persisted, eager hound,
Convinced his day would ultimately dawn,
Did *he* not entertain his hope forlorn.

'Twas Hartley's turn in 1881
To feel a fool (or son of spike-spoiled gun)
When William, first of 'greats', a Renshaw twin
Belaboured Champion straight upon the chin.
Thus Willie brought about a famous coup,
Allowing Hartley to win only two
Of twenty games, 6/0, 6/1, 6/1,
With parson pondering phenomenon.
But p'raps 'tis only fair the truth to state,
And cause for parson's vagaries relate.
No stomach had the vicar for this match
Performed with such irreverent dispatch.
He'd suffered English cholera, poor wretch,
So was unfit to do much else than retch,

Resulting in the briefest final played,
Just thirty-seven minutes undelayed.

The Renshaw twins had started on their reign.
For near ten years it was well-nigh in vain
That rival players sought to strive and strain.
Full seven times did Willie win the title:
And Ernest in the doubles was as vital.
With overhead aplomb, a smashing pair,
Appearing here, there – simply everywhere.

"GAME, SET AND MATCH TO THE RENSHAWS!"

Yes, seven crowns they won, twins' understanding
Well complementing skill quite out-so-standing,
Abetted by meticulous close study
Of all opponents not so fuddy-duddy.

Now played on grass at every country mansion,
The '80s saw lawn tennis-wide expansion
Produce an ever-growing entourage
To watch their heroes' skills and ploys discharge.
So Ernest, Willie too, both handsome idols,
Caused many girls to blush and yearn for bridals.

This personable prepossessing pairing
Attracted more adherents to go airing
On summer afternoons down Worple Road,
To bask in what was now the latest mode.
Old Wimbledon till then still but a village
Began to join the mad rapacious pillage
Of countryside, the population growth
At crazy rate with never sign of sloth.
The rail development had more to do
With populace expansion than a new
Domestic vogue. It stimulated growth,
To which no profiteer was ever loath.
A lease of wicket gate (a pound a year),
Arranged in '69 from railway near,
Allowing access straight into the ground,
In '83 jacked value at a bound.

"SEE WIMBLEDON TENNIS... WORPLE ROAD HALT!"

So many passengers desired alight
As soon as possible to reach the site
And watch their chosen combatants excite,
That Rail allowed a halt at Worple Road,
Where swarms of fans immediately outflowed.
Imagine guards then shouting to exalt,
"See Wimbledon lawn tennis! Worple Halt!"
This privilege endured for quite a time
Until rail tables would no longer chime.

Apart from Renshaws, 1882
Established finally a key review.

The rule that governed height of posts and net
Was altered to contain its potent threat –
Despite the volleyer's profound regret –
To posts three-six, at centre just three feet,
Dimensions ever since declared as meet.

Three times did Ernest win the 'List's' All-Comers
To challenge Willie in clear pristine summers.
He duelled twice for five sets with his twin
And once for four. Alas, he could not win.
He could not?... would not?... that's the teasing question,
But *he* would *never* suffer such suggestion.
He was p'raps right, for like so very many,
Whenever sensing some good hope of any
Near victory, he would oft grow too careful –
A lead to worse, at times becoming fearful –
His natural game then losing all coherence,
Demanding thus the most benign forbearance
From family, dear friends and strong supporters,
Forgetting not their ever-doting daughters.

Year after year the glitt'ring Renshaw crown
Was sought by Lawford just to make his own.
Piratic dog with *a* ferocious forehand
And fiercer spirit, he pursued command.
He never conquered cultivated Willie;
In '87, though, knocked Ernest silly

In final throes of rigorous All-Comers –
A feat that beat his fame among the drummers.
'Twas by default he captured his one title –
For all his skirmishing a just requital –
For Holder, Willie, agonising blow
Occasioned by first case of tennis elbow.

LAWFORD - A PIRATIC DOG WITH
A FEROCIOUS FOREHAND

Canto IV   Regulation and Willie-Nilly

Mid '80s found the courts in sore neglect.
In '85 Herb Lawford did object
To daisies, brought before the whole committee;
While '86 produced a clover – pity
That Herbert Chipp, who plucked it in first round
'Gainst Ernest Renshaw, there no fortune found.
In '83 there'd been initial talk
Of forming an association's caulk
To leaking rules and similar malpractice
And, e'en those days, equivocal play tactics.
So '88 saw LTA's foundation,
Ensuring firm and proper regulation.
Inauguration thus was celebrated
On 26th of Jan, at length debated,
While thirst was quenched and appetite well sated,
Within Freemasons Tavern so select,
With William Renshaw, President elect.

In '88 we find the Renshaw reign
Extended *Ernestly* in fighting vein,
Avenging in the semis signal stain
Of Willie's quarter's loss to Irish 'ghost',
The Will-o-by of Hamilton, with most
Effective forehand, played as running drive,
By which in years to come he'd truly thrive;
But surely haltered now in Ernest's gyve.

All-Comers victor, he contrived to pin
The Holder Lawford in a straight sets win,
Revenge for last year's slight to his dear twin.
But Ernest never won the prize again,
Apparently content with fleeting reign.

So '89 found Renshaw norm resumed
When Willie once again his crown assumed,

"SO AS YOUR FIRST PRESIDENT I GIVE
YOU THE 'LAWN TENNIS ASSOCIATION'!"

As ever Ernest close or runner-up,
And e'er refraining from the sour grapes cup.
Recoup of title was so near denied
To Willie, who was knocked right off his stride
When battling out a fraught All-Comers Final
With Harry Barlow, locked in ding-dong spinal
That had spectators totally enthralled
As Willie sedulously overhauled
A two-set deficit – then stunned… appalled!
A sixth match-point is called and at this crux
Our Willie drops his racket!… Barlow chucks
A sporting lob… With gusto Willie plucks
His racket from the ground and pelts pursuit,
Gyrates and strikes, and perseveres dispute…
Indeed it was a finely forced retrieve
That gave him such fortuitous reprieve.
The final set, though, seemed would soon be Barlow's:
When led 5/0 a punter did propose
A hundred sovereigns 'gainst but one for Willie,
But fortunately found not one so silly
To take his bet and so quite Willie-nilly
He saved his sovereigns – Willie clever winner,
With Barlow rueful, knowing self the sinner.

But ultimately annus '89
Saw *finis* writ beneath the Renshaw line.
In '90 Hamilton came challenge Champion,
Who after three was in the lead 2/1.

By then though, Willie, dead more than alive,
No longer could contain that 'Irish drive'.
'Twas Willoby's sole Wimbledon proud crown,
But Willie's scalp enjoyed unique renown.
This year the Irish won all three events,
A portent p'raps of rude invaders' tents.
In '90, also, new rules for changing ends
At every odd game brought fair dividends.

" CHANGE ENDS! "

The '80s starred a great twin pair of brothers,
The '90s featured conquest by two others.
But first, let's pause, give pattern to the whole,
Relate invasion, revolution's role.
1884 proved a year of change.
The first intruders came to ride the range,
The US Doubles Champions, Dwight and Sears,
Had soon to yield to their Old Country peers.
Three games the Renshaws let the US raiders,
When massacring these innocent crusaders.
Then Ernest/Willie soon re-claimed the crown –
Contested five years since in Oxford Town,
Which they'd attained in '80, '81 –
This first time ever played at Wimbledon.

Canto V   *The Cheshire Kitten – The Legend Comes to Life*

'Twas Henry Jones, again come to the fore,
Proposing ladies should now take the floor,
Who won for them their Singles competition,
(Men's Doubles joining timely recognition).
The field comprised thirteen, including sisters,
Named Watson, Maud and Lilian, both persisters,
Who fought the final, Maud the hard-earned winner.
En route she overcame Blanche Bingley in her
Advance to legend as first Lady Champion.
Next year again Blanche suffered her extinction,
But 1886 saw tables turned
When Blanche, at twenty-two, showed *she'd* fast learned
The vet'ran ploys for which beginners yearned.
Six titles won: it might have been five more,
Had not a tomboy's skill unlocked the door.

She was fourteen, had buffed instinctive game
'Gainst sister and dear brothers, when her fame
Was lit in Bath, defeating Miss Maud Watson,
The Wimbledon First Lady (victor on
A count of fifty-five preceding matches),
So earning just remark in these despatches.
Her name was Lottie Dod, a Cheshire kitten,
Whose Worple coming out had watchers smitten
With disbelief. So gifted was this maiden,
Spectators, players, all alike stayed on

" HERE PUSS ! "

To witness talent such as she'd been given:
Their fascination would have e'en forgiven
If her sweet face with wide grin had been riven
The cat replete with full proverbial cream,
In modern parlance 'playing like a dream'.
Now family lawn tennis might seem well,
But Lottie's aim was always to excel.
A goal was sought. The common-sense way wile
For any youngster was to ape a style.
What better models than the 'smashing' Renshaws,
Whose play was greeted with prolonged applause?
So Lottie had performed th'undreamt till then:
She'd started all-court tennis like the men.
Not serving overhead (that she deplored
As wasting energy) she mainly scored
With forehand, volley and convincing smash,
Her play so startling that she cut a dash.
She beat Blanche Bingley in year '87,
Thus youngest Champion ever seen to leaven
Expansion of this greatest court game show,
Her silken touch too much for calico,
The stuff of gloves pure white Blanche always wore.
Then '88 saw Lottie's first encore.

Next year she went a-yachting, yielding crown
To Blanche, recouping what was once her own
Against L. Rice, a Tipperary girl –
Unknown till she and Blanche prised out a pearl

Encounter. Set, 5/3, 40/15! –
Were Lena's points to be the Worple Queen:
But that was peak of luck's unstable seesaw.
Blanche, resolute, had soon relocked the door.
But '90 found Miss Lena's claim come good.
With Blanche and Lottie both away, she could
Achieve the goal for which she'd nobly sparred.
'Twas from one foursome entry that she starred.
No matter, she returned to home well pleased,
Content with prize that she at last had seized.
She'd roamed 'a long way' from her lone eyrie:
Now back to distant nest in Tipperary.

'91, '92, '93 – all
Were vict'ry years for Dod at pride's recall.
In each her victim Blanche (now Mrs Hillyard),
Who'd married a commander, later guard
Of Wimbledon's true tenets, really great
Club Secret'ry preserving its good state.
'Tis true the fields then battled in were sparse
(The largest nine), so was it all a farce?
The answer's 'No', for many a fine player
Found Lottie's skill soon made efficient slayer –
Like Mo and Lenglen never once defeated,
Every opponent easily unseated,
Save Blanche who took a set at their last meeting
In '93, when Lottie was completing

Her Wimbledon reign. She now sought perfection
Of wider scope and varying complexion.

So Lottie started her all-round career
And burnished eminence already clear.
This time no yachting, rather winter sports
At Moritz, Saint and Queen of Swiss resorts.
Among the first girls riding down the Cresta,
At skating there were few could ever best her.

'Twas in a cricket match peformed on skates
At one of those apocryphal 'blood' dates
Between arch rivals, maidens of Davos
And those of Moritz, right up on her toes,
Our heroine's first bowling spell so brutal
Took five for four, the opposition footle.
She played for England's hockey team in nine-
Ty nine and 1900 – next to shine
At golf. In year '04 competing Troon,
She drove all foes before her, very soon
Had seized the title and so wore the cröwn.
At archery her normal strike was gold –
Her many deeds and prowess often told.
Thereto there'd been none able so comport
With brilliant mastery at every sport.

The men saw '91 vie Erin skill,
In guise of Doctor Pim, oppose its pill
'Gainst Baddeley court-craft of elder twin.
T'was Wilfred who did fashion *his* first win,
Inveigling Pim into prime errors vital
In chase of such a captivating title;
For Pim was known to be perfectionist,
Believing need raised corresponding grist,
So found it unattractive to resist
The ideal stroke that would produce a winner.
Though skilful, Wilfred was beside a spinner

Of wily webs and played on Pim's impatience.
Aware of his impulsive preference,
Doc fought to bridle first instinctive ploy
That frequently so failed to bring him joy.
He duelled Wilfred four full fierce encounters
In finals, giving fans first-rate account as
Advantage waxed for one or then for tother,
While both in turn attempted just to smother
Consummate tactic or outstanding art,
The one to other cogent counterpart.

Thus Baddeley won '91 and '2
But '93 and '4 brought Pim his due.
Next year, Pim not defending, Baddeley
Was given two walk-overs and so he
Faced Aussie Eaves and straight sets dire defeat.
Match-point! Eaves lobbed in bid to join élite…
It fell… out – Baddeley's good luck replete!

In '96 Hal Mahony, Irish too,
Twice beaten by Doc Pim, now battled through
To challenge Wilfred in a 'last chance' duel
Before the Dohertys began their rule.
Poor Wilfred was unfit and not at best,
So Mahony forced attack with hearty zest,
A five sets win, three taken to advantage –
A rightful entry on the Champions' page.

"THIS WAY DARLING!"

'Tis meet here brother Herbert's deeds relate
With Wilfred in the doubles – just first-rate.
Six years they were involved in final round
Whereby four times with title they were crowned.

'Twas during Lottie Dod's and Renshaws' era
That Wimbledon advanced a good step nearer
To matching Lord's as fashionable show,
To which sports followers just had to go.
But entries and real int'rest had declined
Till Dohertys revived them in the mind.

'Twas fitting that two *such* outstanding brothers
Attracted fans when good lacklustre others
Had failed to turn a keen disciple's head,
For they and their skilled sport were born and bred
In that small suburb christened Wimbledon,
A name in wider spheres still barely known –
But not for long. Their play was like a song,
To which spectators turned in growing throng,
Concluding in the '98 fine profit –
Of seventy pounds sterling (nought to scoff at),
In '99 succeeded by two hundred,
A handsome yield indeed to have so plundered;
Result a noble new and smart pavilion
Well suited to the Club's restyled young scion,
'Th'All England Lawn Tennis And Croquet Club',
Predestined as a scintillating cub.

Canto VI   *Ladies to the Forehand*

With Dod's departure from the tennis scene
Blanche set about extending her own reign.
In '94 she had an easy win
But then for two years was not seen again.
The girl who took her chance, Miss Chattie Cooper,
Was soon to prove a true lawn tennis trouper,
Attaining titles five and records two,
Both oldest finalist and winner, too,
One in '08 and tother in '1..2.
So two years running Chattie seized the crown
But on return Blanche Hillyard put her down –
In '97 only after fright,
The first two sets providing fearsome fight.
They were to know each other's game throughout,
For constantly they met in final bout.
The Hillyard qualities were those of pluck
Allied to resolution, shrugging luck,
Her potent stroke a slightly topspun forehand,
With forceful follow-through to give command –
Reluctant volleyer with modest backhand.
Her rival, Chattie, happiest at net
Would volley endlessly to great effect.
She, too, was strong – dexterity her muse –
And enterprising in her net-rush coups.

"GRRRR.....!"

For seven years these two held centre stage
Until a truly great turned Cent'ry's page,
When Dorothea the Douglass fetched her age.

But first '02 saw Muriel steal the scene
And *Robb* poor Chattie of her crown as queen.
Cum match it proved in annals as unique –
The reason was not very far to seek.
Set all, came rain that stopped play for the day.
On morrow match refought from "Love all. Play!"
And Robb it was who had the final say,
Her win deserved, for in her semi's fight
She took the Douglass banner at first sight.
'Twas Dorothea's third bow at Worple Road,
Which soon it seemed she made her own abode.
For Muriel last and culminating year –
She never played again for death was near.

'03, '04 – bench-marks of Douglass fame!
Eleven times she fought her Worple claim
As mistress, Champion seven counts in all
Till year '14 when war proclaimed its thrall
And halcyon days were for ever gone.
For twenty years since Cheshire's Lottie shone
The women's titles seemed 'mongst three foregone –
If neither Blanche nor Chattie, Dorothea
Would take the palm – few others coming near,

Save Muriel late aforenamed, next May flower,
Or Sutton of that ilk, first foreign power
Usurping British right to wear the crown
In '05. Prime attempt at Cent'ry's turn
Had been by Marion Jones, then US Champion,

...SHE TOOK THE DOUGLASS BANNER
AT FIRST SIGHT.

The second round her downfall. Not so May,
A chubby, bright-eyed girl with winning way,
Her country's Champion, too, at seventeen,
Though born in Devon, now a Pasadene,
Had won not only hearts but title too,
For none withstood her forehand follow-through,
Result of speeding at a rapid gallop,
Delivered by a quite tremendous wallop
And even more – with forceful expiration
That seemed to trumpet her anticipation

THAT QUITE TREMENDOUS WALLOP!

BURNING THE WORPLE TURF !

Of winning stroke that even Dorothea,
Upstanding as she was and quite *sans* fear,
Could not deny – like some primeval cry,
Forerunner of the Seles whiplash sigh
More famously renowned as 'Monique's grunt'
Proclaiming that she's really in the hunt!

In 1906 our Dolly had requital
(But only 6/3, 9/7) despite all
Those fearsome forehands. Next year 'twas May's turn
Once more. The forehands sped like fire to burn
The Worple turf. Poor Dolly, Lambert Chambers –
Her marital style – could find no just disclaimers,

Nor stout defence. Spectators were amazed;
For May, well-built as all might see and raised
In California of sunkissed climate,
Had been at birth the healthiest young primate,
An unbelieveable full fifteen pounds,
Inspiring christening congregation's, "Zounds!"

May's chastening of British skill and pride
Was sole success for pre-war foreign tide
On distaff side.
        '08 saw Mrs Sterry
Aged thirty-seven, now create a very
Surprising win against ace Dorothea,
Inflicting then defeat on Dora, dear
Miss Boothby, putting last *la* Morton down
To win her fifth and most distinguished crown,
The oldest victor gaining such renown.

'09 found Chattie resting on her deed,
Inviting Dora Boothby to make speed
And claim the wreath that fate had e'en decreed.
With Mrs Chambers absent, too, it left
An open field to settle who should heft
The cup. Miss Morton proved the final foe,
So she and Dora girt as long ago
For drama to unfold on Worple stage,
Heroic conflict as of classic age,

" ... I'LL SHOW YOU YOUNG 'UNS ! "

A glorious match as both the rivals fought
On... on... and on, the rallies long and taut
Till Dora finally 'came out' at Worple court.

Alas, her reign was short. In 1910
Our Dolly swept through early rounds and then
Allowed the Holder but two games each set.
Next year brave Dora paid a Champion's debt,
Despite a bloodless path to Challenge Round,
Met Dorothea who had no mercy found;
The parson's daughter at her queenly best
To win 6/0, 6/0 with forehand pow'r and zest.
Poor Dora could reflect – if not accord –
On first-time title whitewash to record.

The Douglass once again stood out in '12
To leave the lists, a chance to dig and delve
By one who'd missed five years, now truly seized.
In former days her play had often pleased
As Ethel Thompson when at sister game
Of badminton, she'd made a striking name.
She'd won 'All England' five times out of six.
At Worple Road, too, she'd displayed her tricks.

In 1903, at second try, she'd breached
The bonds of tyro-hood and swiftly reached
The final. Volleys bred of shuttle play
For once had Dolly Douglass in dismay.
Young Ethel took first set to lead the way,
But Douglass steel, well tempered, won the day.
In 1905 she'd lost 8/6, 6/1
In quarters, to May Sutton, only one
To force that Champion to a vantage set.

So Ethel met her greatest challenge yet
(Now Mrs Larcombe, husband who would be,
Like Blanche Hillyard's, a great Club Secretary),
Her victims Hannam, McNair, Hillyard, Sterry,
What roll of tennis stars with which to merry!
These last two great exponents but allowed
Six games between them, e'er they humbly bowed.
'Twas Ethel's finest feat 'fore Worple crowd.

'TWAS ETHEL'S FINEST FEAT!

'13 found Dorothea returned to fray,
Her progress regal as she swept away
Les Tuckey, Morton, Coles and Aitchison
For loss of fifteen games – successful mission!
For Ethel must have thought, "May Heav'n forfend!
What is the point of both'ring to defend?"
'14 saw Ethel take the field again
In second bid to shorten Dolly's reign.
She conquered Chattie, Bunny too, what's more
Forced Dolly to just 7/5, 6/4.
So Dolly Lambert-Chambers held her crown,
A seven-times great Champion of renown.
She wore the diadem just five years more,
An empty honour caused by man-made war.
In 1900 candidates sixteen
Disputed who might rightfully be queen.
1914 brought more than thrice that score.
Full fifty-one came knock upon the door.

The 1880 entry, sixty-one,
Remained the peak attempt by gentlemen,
Declining to sixteen in '87,
Ascending slowly till the Dos' rich leaven
Swelled int'rest in '01 to thirty-seven,
And eighty-five at Dos' end in '07,
1..0..5 by 1911
To pre-war peak one hundred-seventeen,
Arising in the year 1913,

'HIC!' " I SHAY OL' GIRL...'HIC!' LET'SH 'AV A 'MIGSH'D' DOUBLE!"

The same that saw the start of new events,
The Mixed and Ladies' Doubles. This now meant
Five championships accorded new 'World' title
At birth this year of ITF, so vital
To international advance of game.
These titles 'Grass', of course, and yet the same
Acquired by Champions all of Wimbledon,
That name by now to aspirants world known.
The Hard Court titles of the World to France
Were given, theirs the premier tilt of lance
On Riviera courts at play on clay.
These sobriquets stood ten years to the day,
Repealed when US joined the ITF
As price in part of signing up the feoff.

Canto VII   *The Dos and Other Doers*

So now to turn of cent'ry tennis names
That fervent popularity acclaims:
First 'Doherty', aforenamed magic stars,
Both Librans, revelation avatars:
Or so it seemed to eager fans that flocked
To Worple Road, their eyes alive and cocked
To watch their so supremely skilful play
And note the courteous manners they'd display.
The elder, Reggie, soon was dubbed 'Big Do'.
Three years the younger, Laurie, 'Little Do'.
Both Cambridge blues and both unblest in health,
To timing and innate ball sense their wealth
Of rhythmic equilibrium was owed,
Their strokes so strong, from counterpoise they flowed,
Producing maximum effect, delight
That lit agog spectators' eager sight,
Recruiting them as devotees outright.
This pair undoubted as Lawn Tennis saviour,
The Templars of all chivalrous behaviour.

In '94, aged twenty-one, Big Do
First entered Worple lists. He had a go
And reached the doubles final with Hal Nisbet,
In singles took a set off Cazalet.
In '96 he went one better – five
With Mahony while young Laurie did contrive

Four 'gainst Clem Cazalet at first attempt –
To match Big Do. His age though did pre-empt,
For he was only twenty. Had he dreamt
Already future deeds the Dos would do,
Achieving entry in the 'greats' *Who's Who*?

THE MIGHTY AVATARS

That year indeed young Laurie struck a spark,
As first-time finalist to make his mark,
His chance came in 'The Plate', a new event
For early losers, 'Open' luck once spent.
The Do's fine decade turned the century
And killed the penny-pinching penury
Of falling gates. No year was unsubscribed
By Doherty success, the name inscribed
On Champion rolls as reputation bricks
From '97 to 1906.
In '97 Reggie claimed the pyx,
His newly minted crown of sterling win
O'er Wilfred Baddeley, the fount of sin
'Gainst Laurie, Reggie's vengeance sure and swift,
6/3, 6/0, 6/3. He owed some gift
Of fitness to default by F. R. Riseley.
That said, he used advantage very wisely
In first th'All-Comers Final, forcing Eaves –
No quitter – to dead-beat as tallow greaves,
Retiring after two games in the third,
So leaving Reggie finally to gird
For Challenge Round assault on Irish bird,
His conqueror last year. Thus, mem'ry spurred,
Big Do swept through another three sets match
To claim his crown as King of Worple patch.
Between them he and Laurie won eight more,
Their reigns then split by Arthur Wentworth Gore.

But Laurie first in '98 bestrode
All comers, showing Mahony down the road
14/12 in the final set; on way
Beat Hobart, first American to play
A Worple semi-final – not his day.
So Little Do claimed challenge 'gainst Big Do,
The only time the one to tother foe
At Wimbledon. The match endured five sets,
One sole to vantage. Punters made few bets.

THE END OF A MARATHON SESSION

The sense of rivalry was always lacking,
For brother versus brother wished no backing.
Big Do retained the pyx, next year to meet
A. Gore, who in the semis did defeat
Ex-Champion Mahony in a five-set duel,
But 'gainst Big Do could not exert his rule –
Though going five sets. Laurie was that year
Unfit and so in singles failed appear.

In 1900 S. H. Smith made good
To win All-Comers. True, he had withstood
Two early five-set hard-fought rounds beforehand,
Which only served to hone his axe-like forehand.
His final 'gainst last year's survivor, Gore,
Was comfortably garnered in just four.
In challenging Big Do his forehand bludgeon,
Precision-aimed, was miserly curmudgeon
And dominant throughout a long first set,
But tamed thereafter by resilient 'get'
That blunted blade, Reggie the Champion yet.
Though Smith would never be the Worple Champion,
This year he won All England Badminton.

'01 finds twelve-year climber, Arthur Gore,
Who had been pushing firmly to the fore,
With vict'ries over Hillyard in five sets
And Roper Barrett in just four, now net
The last Victorian Champion – also four.

THE TWELVE YEAR CLIMBER

The score to situation does no justice
For Reggie's health had really gone amiss.
He'd hoped that Laurie would A-Cs survive;
Then he'd default, the name thus left alive.
So Reggie played but, leading set, 5/2,
His strength had ebbed too far and he now knew
The time was come to bid the scene *adieu*.

'Twas Reggie's singles swan-song – but not Gore's.
A long career would earn him much applause.

To turn to doubles, here in '96
Big Do and Nisbet ruffed opponents' tricks
To win the right to brave the Baddeleys,
They seized the first two sets but sadly – yes

" TIME PLEASE GENTLEMEN ... DOHERTY
AND NISBET TO SERVE FOR THE MATCH ! "

No more, their challenge spent. Next year the Dos
Combined to earn their claim. They did impose
Defeat, thus taking title, first of eight.
For nine long years but twice did fate negate,
First though a winning sequence to relate.

In '98 and '9 the Dos' defence
Was 'gainst the Anglo/US mixed offence
Of Nisbet/Clarence Hobart, the first Yank
To win a Wimbledon All-Comers rank.
They gained no more, the Dos in firm control,
In modern terms the brothers 'on a roll'.

1900 found challenge from new pair,
Of Roper Barrett, full of doubles flair
And Nisbet. In the semis they first held
The Riseley/Smith alliance but were felled
In five by Dohertys, whose crowns now four.
The fifth was special. In '01 once more
The US Champions, Davis now and Ward
Came tilt in tourney and they swept the board
Till Challenge Round and Dohertys, who floored
Them – only just – 9/7 in the fourth.
Next year the Dos did gird and sally forth,
Returning tilt, achieving straight sets dare
Of US title 'gainst the self-same pair.

The footnote to these conflicts is that Ward –
Defeated in first round by Smith, who scored
Well 'gainst his devilish reverse new serve
That had a mulish kick and break or swerve –
Perplexed the Dos while winning the first set.
They took serve always, even fault or let,
Till confident they'd solved the way to 'get'.

'02 saw Riseley/Smith come at a bound
To make first challenge, prophets to confound
And beat the Dos, cliffhanging win and loss
A-teeter seeming on a coin's toss.
The final score 11/9 in fifth.
Thereafter thrice the Dos allowed scant shrift.
'03, '04 were both in straight sets won,
'05 was harder fought. They ceded one.
'Twas so that Big and Little Do claimed due
As masters at the net, the rival two –
One up, one back – Smith's forehand pow'r from base,
While Riseley's intercepts essayed outface,
At best superb exponents of the art
But Dos in level harness *were* the part.

1906 broke the final fever crisis,
The Dos led 2/1, reached the great abyss.
Big Reggie's health was too much handicap.
He'd never had the strength of rising sap,

MASTERS AT THE NET

While Laurie, p'raps more strong, had not the weight
And sleight, his brother's lack to compensate.
Frank Riseley and Sid Smith had final say
6/3, 6/3 to end their rivals' sway.
The title lost, Big Do did not return
Again to Comers' competition stern.
Indeed, if, under modern rules he'd steeled
Himself to play each year right through the field,
His health would likely have constrained him yield.

When Reggie's grasp failed, Laurie took the torch
Of singles title in '02 to scorch
With athlete's stride his path to tennis fame
And keep a'glitter Dohertys' fair name,
Achieving Champion, only three sets lost,
First two to Mahony, one to Gore the cost.
As Smith and Riseley doubles rivals were,
So singly both were Dohertys' bugbear,
The one had dethroned Reggie once and tother
Was now persistent challenger to brother.
'03, '04 saw Ritchie/Riseley battle
To hold aloft All-Comers' jester's rattle.
F. L. won both. The last by toss was earned
When at 2/2 the pair agreed, 'Adjourned'.
But, challenging, no set could Riseley tease
From Laurie's radiant, easy expertise.

Canto VIII   Wilding and the Wizard

'05 a diff'rent story to relate
For foreign trickle had become a spate,
The entry list contained six nations' names.
The fourth round show comprised two US claims,
Beals Wright and Larned – both with single aims,

A TRICKLE OF FOREIGNERS THAT TURNED TO A SPATE

"GOT ANOTHER ONE MATE!"

Achieved as far as US title went
But never Wimbledon. On quarters' scent
Two Australasians (NZ then was blent),
The Kiwi Wilding and the Aussie Brookes.
Soon both on Worple titles got their hooks.
This was indeed the first attempt by Brookes.
At twenty-seven t'was a late beginnings
But Brookes soon showed he'd have a long-life innings,
With awkward style his racket held short-handed,
The heel pronounced; beside he was left-handed.

And more, he was an arch astute tactician
Superb at volleying and sleight magician
Of service, treacherous with tricky spin
Imparted by reverse and obverse jinn.
Deservedly he earned the name 'The Wizard',
Which stuck in many an opponent's gizzard.

The Wizard had a meteoric start,
Asundering best players, shred apart
By volleys fierce and wily, well-placed smash
With which he'd tentative high-lobs dispatch
And googly serves, whose spinning swerve direction
Were viewed with anxious cross-eyed circumspection.
His splint'ring progress lost him not a set
To final A-C round. En route he met
And conquered Hillyard, Riseley and then Gore.
Some trio claim for tyro's opening score!
He then met Smith of Stroud, whose famous 'punch'
From powered forehand sure must be the crunch.
It was a classic two-style confrontation,
Though fought throughout with great determination,
The score each set uneven, save the last
When Smith's attack propelled by forehand blast
Earned service break but Brookes – no whit aghast –
Recovered loss and won by 7/5.

The Wizard's run caused speculation live.
Could reigning Champion 'Do' contain the drive?

THE 'WIZARD' FROM DOWN UNDER!

Though 'Little' dubbed he had heroic heart.
When led 6/5 he took Brookes' serve apart
To win the match 8/6, 6/2, 6/4,
But vintage tennis was belied by score,
For all the fortunates who saw the game,
As finest ever witnessed did proclaim.
'Twas Laurie's zenith, though he won next year
'Gainst old foe, Riseley. Frank then took good cheer
When he and Smith dethroned 'Do' doubles pair.
It signalled era end for all four players,
Who'd done so much for tennis as purveyors.
But Gore, who'd taken Wilding in the quarters,
Remained for long as senior of disporters.

'06 provided fleeting singles lull
From foreign raiders answ'ring Worple pull.
But next year Brookes was back renewed with zest
And subjugating onslaught in his quest
For world-wide coveted, prize Worple crown
He was intent this time to make his own.
The luck of draw, imperilled by no seeding
Soon brought encounter 'gainst mate Wilding, needing
Five sets to score success. Then three sank Lowe
Before Karl Behr, a Yank, gave blow for blow
In first four sets but none of five to vantage.
That fence behind, Norm surged to final stage,
To doff no mercy to the ageless Gore,
6/0, 6/1, 6/4 the telling score.

Sans Laurie to defend the Champion title,
It was perhaps a slightly vain requital.
The same applied to doubles Challenge Round.
The Dos had gone and good pairs weren't around.
Anachronistic Anzacs, Brookes and Wilding
Went through the field with fierce and fiery sting,
The Yanks, Karl Behr and Wright, lacked moral fight.
They'd lost in singles, Behr to Brookes and Wright
To Wilding. Confidence was put to flight.
A sinister historic note – this first
Of finals being two left-handers cursed.

So Australasia both mens' titles seized,
The first such booty pirated o'erseas.
In 1908 no Brookes again, the field,
Though international, not vintage yield,
A chance for steady vet'ran, Arthur Gore,
To come right through at forty and still score
As oldest Champion, beating Dixon, more
His end-game foe was Roper Barrett, aged
Good thirty-four, the oldest final ever staged –

The doubles skills of Barrett versus base-
Line forehands Gore would pitilessly place
Exact to inch, footwork of grace and pace
Enabling him avoid most backhand strokes,
However sly opponents tried to coax.
In doubles Wilding / Ritchie overthrew
The coupled Gore and Roper Barrett, who
Had beaten both in singles – vengeance coup.
The Anzac, Wilding, who with Brookes joint Holder,
Uniquely needing give himself cold shoulder –
Walk-over self to leave him feeling older.

In 1909 the rain had too much say,
Affecting mood as well as run of play,
Five foreign entrants reached the quarters' frays
But Ritchie fought the Comers' final phase
'Gainst Barrett, beating him in only four,
Then took the floor to challenge Champion Gore.
Though winning first two sets and four years younger,
He could not match the older player's hunger.
That same year Gore acquired first doubles title,
His partner Barrett, whose net play was vital
To complement the baseline driving skills
Of Gore, whose plaguing forehand opened up the kills.

1910. Wilding started his ascension.
Already Doubles Champion, singles mention,

Not writ as yet on title rolls. His climb
Had seen some minor deeds. Now, nearing prime,
He vanquished Barrett, Ritchie and Froitzheim
To reach All-Comers Final versus Wright,
Who'd been his first round victim (three sets tight)
In 1907. Wright though had won twice
In Davis Cup. With fresh sangfroid of ice
The Kiwi stood his ground as Wright's net-rush
Secured two sets. Then strength began to gush
Away, until no longer had he sway
And soon was forced to calling it a day.
Now came the challenge. Champion, Arthur Gore,
Had been his victor twice in years before.
None yet would ever think to take Gore light.
At forty-two, he still put up a fight,
Led 4/1 in the first and took the third,
But Wilding knew he had the chance. So spurred,
He raised his game and justly claimed his crown.
Rejoining Ritchie, they then went to town,
Their only fight 'gainst Doust and Poidevin,
Both Aussies, *theirs* though *final* will to win.
The Challenge Round the most one-sided yet –
Four games were all that Barrett/Gore could nett.

Canto IX   *Heavenly Wonders and the Wizard's Spell*

1911, largest entry yet.
1..0..4 chanced the draw's roulette,
The French in force and other continentals,
The British of all kinds and detrimentals.
The old 'uns' still progressed to later stages,
Experience having given them good gauges,

By which to judge opponents and their skills.
Decugis, Dixon, Barrett, Lowe (no frills)
Were semis line-up. Dixon, thirty-eight,
And Barrett, thirty-seven, gave the gate
Good value for their money under sun
Of broiling heat, the match prolonged – not one
For frailty. Dixon took the first two sets
At cost to energy. The punters' bets
Were still on Barrett whittling back the lead,
And finally 'twas he that did succeed.
The Challenge Round appeared as if repeat;
For Barrett, ten more sere, seemed might unseat
The Champion when he led two sets to one.
But Wilding caught him and he was undone,
The weariness of chance he'd lost and age
Main factors in retirement at this stage.

The same year France's maiden pair appearance
Attained All-Comers' end – with perseverance.
Decugis'/Gobert's net attack was fierce
Their trenchant volleys mordantly did pierce.
The first three rounds were taken in their stride;
The next they found to be a rougher ride.
In semis Aussies Pockley and Stan Doust
Did give the French fair dinkum five-set joust.
The Challenge Round was not an easy picnic,
For Holders Ritchie/Wilding did fast stick,

Unwilling yield their title as of right,
Resulting in another five sets fight.
The French at last won *concours d'élégance*
But not before they'd tripped a merry dance.

In 1912 return of Roper Barrett,
This time with lawyer Dixon off'ring carrot

"ANYONE FOR TENNIS?"

Of partnership prolific in its titles,
The one to tother giving fair requitals.
They won A-C 'gainst Beamish/J. C. Parke,
Who first beat Doust and Wilding, making mark.
Now Parke, a famous Irish rugby man,
At tennis was in *no* way 'also ran'.
The Anglo-Irish duo led 2/1
In sets. Not many bets 'gainst them were done,
But final score gave senior pair the edge,
Their canny combination forming kedge.

In Challenge Round Decugis and Gobert
Began well, demonstrating Gallic flair,
Were forced at end to yield to elder pair,
Who 'tween them carried well-nigh eighty years,
Part due no doubt to vigorous forbears.
'13 saw seniors fight off German foe,
Their first to reach the cut-throat challenge throe.
When Kleinschroth/Rahe vanquished Beamish/Parke
In semis many backed their big-gunned barque,
To broadside Champions, giving better fight
Than French last year. The seniors took it light,
Their score 3/1, joint 'handicap' plus forty,
A dangerous age, 'tis said, if feeling naughty.

But now to serious matters, singles throne
In '12 disputed by the French and own.

In semis Gore did better Beamish boy,
While Gobert and Decugis, using Troy
As standard 'gainst all subterfugal ploy,
Did wrestle each the other might and main:
The younger, Gobert, better stood the strain,
Surviving 6/4 in the fifth, to meet
Grey Gore. The youngster Gobert he did beat
3/1 – a most considerable feat.
He lost his challenge to the Holder, Tony
The Wilding, but who would have bet a pony

"ZO HANS... MIT DIE FÜRST SERVICE BALL...
..ICH LODEN ZE BIG BARKING GUN YA!"

On any other end? The fact remains
That Gore and Sterry had similar campaigns.
In this one year both he and Chattie Sterry
Acquired the same fine record, each the veri-
Est oldest Champion, also runner-up.
Indeed they drank from heroes' brimming cup.

1913 was comet year of presage
With looming war perhaps as plainest message.
But comets with split tails are sometimes met
And one tail told the best of stories yet
Of 'Californian Comet' come to get
The highest prize, on which his heart was set.

" YEEHAA! ... WORPLE ROAD AND HERE
COMES THE CALIFORNIAN COMET ! "

RAT-A-TAT-TAT! IT'S THE ROPER DOUBLE SHOOTER

His stature tall with dominating reach,
An athlete's grace, good balance, cling of leech,
His movements those of innate ballet dancer,
Nijinsky gifted with each tennis answer.

The Challenge Round found Patterson now starting
As if from last year there had been no parting.
Straight into form, he led set and 3/0
Before Big Bill found touch and made his move –
A run of six straight games to square the match
And from the coils sweet victory to snatch.
Once in his stride he nevermore let up,
The winner by 3/1 to take the cup.

Big Bill not only won first Wimbledon
But was as well first male American
To gain that cherished prize.
                              In '21,
To be last Challenge Round and Worple year,
Came entries flooding from just everywhere,
For Wimbledon was now pre-eminent
Among world's championships. Acceptance meant
Admittance to élitist brotherhood –
The best that tennis now considered good.

One quarter-final was the strangest yet
'Twixt Shimidzu and sturdy Randolph Lycett,
Who, labouring in throes of hard-fought game,
Renewed his energies with iced champagne,
Enhanced, t'was said, with brandy 'gainst all drain.
The match proved long and very strenuous,
The vantage always finely tenuous.

" CHEERS UMP! 'AV A BLASS OF `HIC!` GUBBLY
'OL BOY... AN' YOU TOO SHMEE...SSHIDZU `NO..`
SHIMZIMDOO `HIC!` ! "

The last few games revealed a reeling Lycett
Somehow contrive to stay alive in set,
While Shimidzu and umpire both refrained
From any interchange that might offend.
The Japanese was winner by 10/8,
With Randolph focusing on walking straight.
He must have talked at length with Lenglen's pa,
Who, we shall see, provided his own bar.

The Final round was ultimately won
By new contestant, Brian called 'Boy' Norton,
A twenty-one year old South African
Whose great potential and star talent shone.
He now by right came up against the Champion
In bid to seize the coveted king's crown.

The Boy's success was well deserved, if lucky,
In A-C final he'd subdued the plucky
Alonso, who was utterly worn out
From meeting Shimidzu in five-set bout,
Last score 8/6 but always in some doubt.
Against the Boy, Alonso started well,
Was leading two love 5/2 till the knell
Of tiredness struck and thus the Boy went through
To Challenge Round and there 'a nice to do'!

So come encounter day and straight we find
The Boy at once into his stroke, his mind

It poured and poured till cry "Abandon play",
The wretched rivals left to prowl all day.

Next day found wholly splendid shining morn,
All innocence as if repentant dawn.
There was no wind, the court as always true.
The Champion felt instinctively she knew
Her form would match such stimulant occasion,
Crusader new against the proven bastion.
So under winsome sun and wisps above
Suzanne served first and lost the game to love;
But then recouped to lead four games to one
And 5/3, set-point but Dorothea soon
Salved that with two superb drop-shots and then
Led 6/5 and two set-points herself, when
Suzanne denied her by her steadfast play.
The battle raged in strong pulsating sway –
A love game each then fast, fine, furious fray
That climaxed with Suzanne ahead 10/8,
Her final stroke a drop-volley played late –
A strike of genius. But of the two
It was surprisingly the younger who
Appeared distressed, a spur to grand old Champion.
She reached 4/1, whereon *cher* Papa Lenglen
Cast down a tiny flask, liquidity –
Supreme essence, a mighty quiddity.
No sooner drained, Suzanne attacked anew.
4/4 soon came before the Champion drew

"COME ON SUZANNE ... I'M FREEZING!"

On hidden depths to take the set 6/4.
Suzanne then asked for brandy and what's more
Requested linesman's chair, whereon she sat
While Dorothea, unsure what she was at,
Was getting chilled. So when the game resumed
Suzanne was soon 4/1, the Champion doomed,
Or so it seemed. She'd been somewhat annoyed
By vile net-cords but firmed her mind, was buoyed
To square the set. Each then accrued love game.
5/5. There followed rallies fierce e'er claim
Was trumpeted. 6/5, 40/15.
Thought Dorothea, "So now it will be seen
By doubting fools, who now is still the queen!"

AND THAT, YOUR MAJESTY, IS THE ROLLER END

ENVOI

Decision Days

When the Queen of the realm decides to stay,
But the King of tennis calls it a day,
"Oh, I say! Oh, I say!"

Now Maskell has quit the commentary box
The rest will have to pull up their socks,
Or take a few knocks - quite a few knocks.

How to compete with a living legend?
There's only one way. You take the pledge and…
Now where do you stand? Where do you stand?

Well, you do your homework - six hours a day,
And then you go out and describe the play.
"Oh, I say! Oh, I say!'

Cap Ferrat
7th February 1992

The above light lines were occasioned at the beginning of February 1992, by first the Queen announcing that she would not be abdicating after forty years and a week later Dan Maskell announcing his retirement.

To Fred Perry
1905-1995

You heard the siren call of ball on string,
So dared to scale the wall of Devon Park;
You stared as white-clad figures made their mark
And knew your heart was lost and soul would sing.

You leapt the barricades of barren 'form'
And strode the tennis courts in conqu'ring mode.
For you the goal was set and straight the road,
The rule to fight with gut and *not* conform.

Your chafing spirit seized its proud reward
As overlord supreme among our champions,
Receiving all the plaudits and the paeans -
Thrice-running victor on All England sward.

You stand there rightful guardian of the shrine:
May patriotic fame be ever thine.

Aldbourne
2nd February 1995

*Written on the day Fred Perry died, and printed in the order of
his memorial service at St Paul's.*

Milestones at Worple Road

1868-69   All England Croquet Club formed with rented grounds at Worple Road.

1869   Lease of wicket gate from the Railway into clubs' grounds.

1871   Pony-roller presented to club by John Walsh, Editor-in-Chief *The Field*, in return for his daughter having free membership.

1872   Major Harry Gem and J. B. Perera play a racket game on their lawns at Leamington.

1873   Major Clopton Wingfield introduces 'sphairistike' – his boxed garden pastime – during a December weekend at Nantclywd.

1875   The All England Croquet Club starts lawn tennis.

1877   Club's name is changed (14th April) to embrace the new sport. First Lawn Tennis Championships take place. The net, following Real tennis, is 5' at the posts and 3' 3" at the centre.

1878   Over-arm service made legal.
Hadow wins title at first attempt without losing a set – the first time ever done. Never enters again.
Net and posts reduced by three inches.

1880   The service let introduced.

1882   Net lowered to 3'6" at posts and 3' at centre, the standard ever since.

1883   Railway company allows a Halt at Worple Road during Championships, a privilege that lasted several years.

1884   First Ladies' Singles Championships
Men's Doubles, previously contested at Oxford from 1879, played at Wimbledon for the first time.
First overseas entries, Dwight and Sears, US doubles champions.

1887   William Renshaw does not defend his title, due to first recorded case of tennis elbow.
Lottie Dod wins Ladies' Singles at her first attempt, the youngest Champion ever at 15 years 285 days.

1888	LTA founded on 26th January, with William Renshaw as President.
1890	The rule introduced for changing ends after each odd game of a set.
1893	Lottie Dod wins fifth title and retires unbeaten, aged 20, to conquer other sports.
1896	The Plate competition introduced.
1899	A new pavilion built as a result of a £200 profit. Club re-styled The All England Lawn Tennis and Croquet Club.
1902	Ladies' Challenge Round rained off at set all and replayed from love all next day, the only time this has ever happened.
1905	US Champion, May Sutton, becomes the first overseas winner of any title.
1907	Australian Norman Brookes, 'The Wizard', wins the Singles and, partnered by New Zealander Tony Wilding, the Doubles – the first time either Men's title went overseas.
1908	Mrs Sterry (Chattie Cooper) takes her fifth title as oldest winner, aged 37 years, 282 days.
1909	Arthur Gore takes his third singles title, aged 40 years 182 days, the oldest Men's Singles winner.
1910	Holder Mrs Lambert Chambers beats challenger Dora Boothby 6/0, 6/0 – only whitewash to date in a singles final.
1911	France wins her first Wimbledon title in the Men's Doubles with Decugis and Gobert.
1913	Start of Ladies' and Mixed Doubles. ITF founded. Wimbledon given the title of 'The World Championships on Grass', Paris 'The World Hard Court Championships'.
1919	Bill Tilden wins Men's Singles – the first American man to win any Wimbledon title. Suzanne Lenglen, aged 20, wins her first of six singles titles, the first singles champion for France.
1921	Last year the Championships are played at Worple Road. Last year of the Challenge Round.
1922	First Championships at Church Road.

The Results of Championships played at Worple Road

In all the Championships at Worple Road (1877-1921), except the first, the main tournament (The All-Comers) was played to determine who would win the right to play against the Champion in the Challenge Round, which decided the title. In years when the Holder did not defend, the winner of the All-Comers' Final 'walked-over' in the Challenge Round and automatically became the new Champion. In the tables that follow, the first match listed against each year is the All-Comers' Final and the second is the Challenge Round. Where there is only one match listed, the Holder did not defend.

Men's Singles

Year	Winner	Runner-up	Score
1877	S.W. Gore	W.C. Marshall	6/1, 6/2, 6/4
1878	P.F. Hadow	L.R. Erskine	6/4, 6/4, 6/4
	P.F. Hadow	S.W. Gore	7/5, 6/1, 9/7
1879	J.T. Hartley	V.T. St Leger Goold	6/2, 6/4, 6/2
1880	H.F. Lawford	O.E. Woodhouse	7/5, 6/4, 6/0
	J.T. Hartley	H.F. Lawford	6/3, 6/2, 2/6, 6/3
1881	W.C. Renshaw	R.T. Richardson	6/4, 6/2, 6/3
	W.C. Renshaw	J.T. Hartley	6/0, 6/1, 6/1
1882	J.E. Renshaw	R.T. Richardson	7/5, 6/3, 2/6, 6/3
	W.C. Renshaw	J.E. Renshaw	6/1, 2/6, 4/6, 6/2, 6/2
1883	J.E. Renshaw	D.C. Stewart	0/6, 6/3, 6/0, 6/2
	W.C. Renshaw	J.E. Renshaw	2/6, 6/3, 6/3, 4/6, 6/3
1884	H.F. Lawford	C.W. Grinstead	7/5, 2/6, 6/2, 9/7
	W.C. Renshaw	H.F. Lawford	6/0, 6/4, 9/7
1885	H.F. Lawford	J.E. Renshaw	5/7, 6/1, 0/6, 6/2, 6/4
	W.C. Renshaw	H.F. Lawford	7/5, 6/2, 4/6, 7/5
1886	H.F. Lawford	E.W. Lewis	6/2, 6/3, 2/6, 4/6, 6/4
	W.C. Renshaw	H.F. Lawford	6/0, 5/7, 6/3, 6/4
1887	H.F. Lawford	J.E. Renshaw	1/6, 6/3, 3/6, 6/4, 6/4
1888	J.E. Renshaw	E.W. Lewis	7/9, 6/1, 8/6, 6/4
	J.E. Renshaw	H.F. Lawford	6/3, 7/5, 6/0

Year	Winner	Runner-up	Score
1889	W.C. Renshaw	H.S. Barlow	3/6, 5/7, 8/6, 10/8, 8/6
	W.C. Renshaw	J.E. Renshaw	6/4, 6/1, 3/6, 6/0
1890	W.J. Hamilton	H.S. Barlow	2/6, 6/4, 6/4, 4/6, 7/5
	W.J. Hamilton	W.C. Renshaw	6/8, 6/2, 3/6, 6/1, 6/1
1891	W. Baddeley	J. Pim	6/4, 1/6, 7/5, 6/0
1892	J. Pim	E.W. Lewis	2/6, 5/7, 9/7, 6/3, 6/2
	W. Baddeley	J. Pim	4/6, 6/3, 6/3, 6/2
1893	J. Pim	H.S. Mahony	9/7, 6/3, 6/0
	J. Pim	W. Baddeley	3/6, 6/1, 6/3, 6/2
1894	W. Baddeley	E.W. Lewis	6/0, 6/1, 6/0
	J. Pim	W. Baddeley	10/8, 6/2, 8/6
1895	W. Baddeley	W.V. Eaves	4/6, 2/6, 8/6, 6/2, 6/3
1896	H.S. Mahony	W.V. Eaves	6/2, 6/2, 11/9
	H.S. Mahony	W. Baddeley	6/2, 6/8, 5/7, 8/6, 6/3
1897	R.F. Doherty	W.V. Eaves	6/3, 7/5, 2/0 retd
	R.F. Doherty	H.S. Mahony	6/4, 6/4, 6/3
1898	H.L. Doherty	H.S. Mahony	6/1, 6/2, 4/6, 2/6, 14/12
	R.F. Doherty	H.L. Doherty	6/3, 6/3, 2/6, 5/7, 6/1
1899	A.W. Gore	S.H. Smith	3/6, 6/2, 6/1, 6/4
	R.F. Doherty	A.W. Gore	1/6, 4/6, 6/3, 6/3, 6/3
1900	S.H. Smith	A.W. Gore	6/4, 4/6, 6/2, 6/1
	R.F. Doherty	S.H. Smith	6/8, 6/3, 6/1, 6/2
1901	A.W. Gore	C.P. Dixon	6/4, 6/0, 6/3
	A.W. Gore	R.F. Doherty	4/6, 7/5, 6/4, 6/4
1902	H.F. Doherty	M.J.G. Ritchie	8/6, 6/3, 7/5
	H.L. Doherty	A.W. Gore	6/4, 6/3, 3/6, 6/0
1903	F.L. Riseley	M.J.G. Ritchie	1/6, 6/3, 8/6, 13/11
	H.L. Doherty	F.L. Riseley	7/5, 6/3, 6/0
1904	F.L. Riseley	M.J.G. Ritchie	6/0, 6/1, 6/2
	H.L. Doherty	F.L. Riseley	6/1, 7/5, 8/6
1905	N.E. Brookes	S.H. Smith	1/6, 6/4, 6/1, 1/6, 7/5
	H.L. Doherty	N.E. Brookes	8/6, 6/2, 6/4
1906	F.L. Riseley	A.W. Gore	6/3, 6/3, 6/4
	H.L. Doherty	F.L. Riseley	6/4, 4/6, 6/2, 6/3
1907	N.E. Brookes	A.W. Gore	6/4, 6/2, 6/2
1908	A.W. Gore	H. Roper Barrett	6/3, 6/2, 4/6, 3/6, 6/4
1909	M.J.G. Ritchie	H. Roper Barrett	6/2, 6/3, 4/6, 6/4
	A.W. Gore	M.J.G. Ritchie	6/8, 1/6, 6/2, 6/2, 6/2

Year	Winner	Runner-up	Score
1910	A.F. Wilding	B.C. Wright	4/6, 4/6, 6/3, 6/2, 6/3
	A.F. Wilding	A.W. Gore	6/4, 7/5, 4/6, 6/2
1911	H. Roper Barrett	C.P. Dixon	5/7, 4/6, 6/4, 6/3, 6/1
	A.F. Wilding	H. Roper Barrett	6/4, 4/6, 2/6, 6/2 retd
1912	A.W. Gore	A.H. Gobert	9/7, 2/6, 7/5, 6/1
	A.F. Wilding	A.W. Gore	6/4, 6/4, 4/6, 6/4
1913	M.E. McLoughlin	S.N. Doust	6/3, 6/4, 7/5
	A.F. Wilding	M.E. McLoughlin	8/6, 6/3, 10/8
1914	N.E. Brookes	O. Froitzheim	6/2, 6/1, 5/7, 4/6, 8/6
	N.E. Brookes	A.F. Wilding	6/4, 6/4, 7/5
1915-18	No competition		
1919	G.L. Patterson	A.R.F. Kingscote	6/2, 6/1, 6/3
	G.L. Patterson	N.E. Brookes	6/3, 7/5, 6/2
1920	W.T. Tilden	Z. Shimidzu	6/4, 6/4, 13/11
	W.T. Tilden	G.L. Patterson	2/6, 6/3, 6/2, 6/4
1921	B.I.C. Norton	M. Alonso	5/7, 4/6, 7/5, 6/3, 6/3
	W.T. Tilden	B.I.C. Norton	4/6, 2/6, 6/1, 6/0, 7/5

Ladies' Singles

Year	Winner	Runner-up	Score
1884	Miss M.E.E. Watson	Miss L.M. Watson	6/8, 6/3, 6/3
1885	Miss M.E.E. Watson	Miss B. Bingley	6/1, 7/5
1886	Miss B. Bingley	Miss A. Tabor	6/2, 6/0
	Miss B. Bingley	Miss M.E.E. Watson	6/3, 6/3
1887	Miss C. Dod	Mrs C.J. Cole	6/2, 6/3
	Miss C. Dod	Miss B. Bingley	6/2, 6/0
1888	Mrs G.W. Hillyard	Miss Howes	6/1, 6/2
	Miss C. Dod	Mrs G.W. Hillyard	6/3, 6/3
1889	Mrs G.W. Hillyard	Miss H.G.B. Rice	4/6, 8/6, 6/4
1890	Miss H.G.B. Rice	Miss M. Jacks	6/4, 6/1
1891	Miss C. Dod	Mrs G.W. Hillyard	6/2, 6/1
1892	Mrs G.W. Hillyard	Miss E.M. Shackle	6/1, 6/4
	Miss C. Dod	Mrs G.W. Hillyard	6/1, 6/1
1893	Mrs G.W. Hillyard	Miss E.M. Shackle	6/3, 6/2
	Miss C. Dod	Mrs G.W. Hillyard	6/8, 6/1, 6/4
1894	Mrs G.W. Hillyard	Miss E.L. Austin	6/1, 6/1
1895	Miss C.R. Cooper	Miss H. Jackson	7/5, 8/6

Year	Winner	Runner-up	Score
1896	Mrs W.H. Pickering	Miss E.L. Austin	4/6, 6/3, 6/3
	Miss C.R. Cooper	Mrs W.H. Pickering	6/2, 6/3
1897	Mrs G.W. Hillyard	Mrs W.H. Pickering	6/2, 7/5
	Mrs G.W. Hillyard	Miss C.R. Cooper	5/7, 7/5, 6/2
1898	Miss C.R. Cooper	Miss M.L. Martin	6/4, 6/4
1899	Mrs G.W. Hillyard	Mrs N.J. Durlacher	7/5, 6/8, 6/1
	Mrs G.W. Hillyard	Miss C.R. Cooper	6/2, 6/3
1900	Miss C.R. Cooper	Miss M.L. Martin	8/6, 5/7, 6/1
	Mrs G.W. Hillyard	Miss C.R. Cooper	4/6, 6/4, 6/4
1901	Mrs A. Sterry	Miss M.L. Martin	6/3, 6/4
	Mrs A. Sterry	Mrs G.W. Hillyard	6/2, 6/2
1902	Miss M.E. Robb	Miss A.M. Morton	6/2, 6/4
	Miss M.E. Robb	Mrs A. Sterry	7/5, 6/1
1903	Miss D.K. Douglass	Miss E.W. Thomson	4/6, 6/4, 6/2
1904	Mrs A. Sterry	Miss A.M. Morton	6/3, 6/3
	Miss D.K. Douglass	Mrs A. Sterry	6/0, 6/3
1905	Miss M.G. Sutton	Miss C.M. Wilson	6/3, 8/6
	Miss M.G. Sutton	Miss D.K. Douglass	6/3, 6/4
1906	Miss D.K. Douglass	Mrs A. Sterry	6/2, 6/2
	Miss D.K. Douglass	Miss M.G. Sutton	6/3, 9/7
1907	Miss M.G. Sutton	Miss C.M. Wilson	6/4, 6/2
	Miss M.G. Sutton	Mrs Lambert Chambers	6/1, 6/4
1908	Mrs A. Sterry	Miss A.M. Morton	6/4, 6/4
1909	Miss P.D.H. Boothby	Miss A.M. Morton	6/4, 4/6, 8/6
1910	Mrs Lambert Chambers	Miss E.G. Johnson	6/4, 6/2
	Mrs Lambert Chambers	Miss P.D.H. Boothby	6/2, 6/2
1911	Miss P.D.H. Boothby	Mrs F.J. Hannam	6/2, 7/5
	Mrs Lambert Chambers	Miss P.D.H. Boothby	6/0, 6/0
1912	Mrs D.T.R. Larcombe	Mrs A. Sterry	6/3, 6/1
1913	Mrs Lambert Chambers	Mrs R.J. McNair	6/0, 6/4
1914	Mrs D.T.R. Larcombe	Miss E.M. Ryan	6/3, 6/2
	Mrs Lambert Chambers	Mrs D.T.R. Larcombe	7/5, 6/4
1915-18	No competition		
1919	Miss S.R.F. Lenglen	Mrs C.R. Satterthwaite	6/1, 6/1
	Miss S.R.F. Lenglen	Mrs Lambert Chambers	10/8, 4/6, 9/7
1920	Mrs Lambert Chambers	Miss E.M. Ryan	6/2, 6/1
	Miss S.R.F. Lenglen	Mrs Lambert Chambers	6/3, 6/0
1921	Miss E.M. Ryan	Mrs C.R. Satterthwaite	6/1, 6/0
	Miss S.R.F. Lenglen	Miss E.M. Ryan	6/2, 6/0

Men's Doubles
Results of the Challenge Rounds only
(* played at Oxford)

Year	Champions	Runners-up	Score
1879*	L.R. Erskine and H.F. Lawford	F. Durant and G.E. Tabor	6/4, 6/5, 6/2, 3/6, 5/6, 10/8
1880*	W.C. Renshaw and J.E. Renshaw	O.E. Woodhouse and C.J. Cole	6/1, 6/4, 6/0, 6/8, 6/3
1881*	W.C. Renshaw and J.E. Renshaw	W.J. Down and H. Vaughan	6/0, 6/0, 6/4
1882*	J.T. Hartley and R.T. Richardson	J.G. Horn and C.B. Russell	6/2, 6/1, 6/0
1883*	C.W. Grinstead and C.E. Welldon	C.B. Russell and R.T. Milford	3/6, 6/1, 6/3, 6/4
1884	W.C. Renshaw and J.E. Renshaw	E.W. Lewis and E.L. Williams	6/3, 6/1, 1/6, 6/4
1885	W.C. Renshaw and J.E. Renshaw	C.E. Farrar and A.J. Stanley	6/3, 6/3, 10/8
1886	W.C. Renshaw and J.E. Renshaw	C.E. Farrar and A.J. Stanley	6/3, 6/3, 4/6, 7/5
1887	H.W.W. Wilberforce and Hon P.B. Lyon	J.H. Crispe and E Barratt Smith	7/5, 6/3, 6/2
1888	W.C. Renshaw and J.E. Renshaw	H.W.W. Wilberforce and Hon P.B. Lyon	2/6, 1/6, 6/3, 6/4, 6/3
1889	W.C. Renshaw and J.E. Renshaw	E.W. Lewis and G.W. Hillyard	6/4, 6/4, 3/6, 0/6, 6/1
1890	J. Pim and F.O. Stoker	E.W. Lewis and G.W. Hillyard	6/0, 7/5, 6/4
1891	W. Baddeley and H. Baddeley	J. Pim and F.O. Stoker	6/1, 6/3, 1/6, 6/2
1892	E.W. Lewis and H.S. Barlow	W. Baddeley and H. Baddeley	4/6, 6/2, 8/6, 6/4
1893	J. Pim and F.O. Stoker	E.W. Lewis and H.S. Barlow	4/6, 6/3, 6/1, 2/6, 6/0
1894	W. Baddeley and H. Baddeley	H.S. Barlow and C.H. Martin	5/7, 7/5, 4/6, 6/3, 8/6
1895	W. Baddeley and H. Baddeley	E.W Lewis and W.V. Eaves	8/6, 5/7, 6/4, 6/3
1896	W. Baddeley and H. Baddeley	R.F. Doherty and H.A. Nisbet	1/6, 3/6, 6/4, 6/2, 6/1